VICO'S THEORY
OF THE CAUSES OF
HISTORICAL CHANGE

Leon Pompa, M.A., Ph.D.

1971
(Revised 1998)

MONOGRAPH SERIES NO. 1

The Institute for Cultural Research

ISBN 978-1-78479-360-9

First published 1971
Published in this edition 2019

Requests for permission to reprint, reproduce etc., to:
The Permissions Department
ISF Publishing
The Idries Shah Foundation
P. O. Box 71911
London NW2 9QA
United Kingdom
permissions@isf-publishing.org

In association with The Idries Shah Foundation

The Idries Shah Foundation is a registered charity in
the United Kingdom
Charity No. 1150876

The Author

LEON POMPA WAS Professor of Philosophy, 1977-1997 (now Professor Emeritus), in the University of Birmingham. His many publications include: *Vico: A study of the 'New Science'* (Cambridge University Press, 1975; revised and enlarged, CUP, 1990); *Vico: Selected writings*, ed. and trans. (CUP, 1982); *Human Nature and Historical Knowledge: Hume, Hegel and Vico* (CUP, 1990; first paperback ed. CUP, 2002); *Vico: The First New Science*, ed. and trans. (CUP, 2002).

This monograph is a transcript of a lecture delivered to the Institute for Cultural Research on 17th October, 1970.

Vico's Theory of the Causes of Historical Change

I AM GOING to try this evening to bring out certain aspects of the thought of the Italian philosopher, Giambattista Vico, which can help us in trying to understand what people sometimes call 'our human condition'. I shall not be concerned so much to show that these theories are true or false, as to show that they open up interesting and profitable ways of thinking about ourselves and the situation we are in.

I shall begin by saying something fairly brief about Vico himself, because he is not a philosopher who attracted very much attention until he was rediscovered first by the great French historian, Michelet, in the 19th century, and then by the Italian philosopher, Croce, and his successors in this century. But even so, interest in him has largely remained confined to Italy. There are a number of reasons for this but I'm not going to go into them except to say that, in the end, it is the sheer obscurity of his writings that has stood as a barrier to any general interest in his thought.

The events of Vico's life make a very unexciting story. He was born in 1668 in Naples, the son of a bookseller. And, apart from a few years spent as tutor to a Cardinal's nephew at a place just outside Naples, he never left there. He died in 1744, in the same year that the final and most complete version of his greatest work, the *New Science* was published. For most of his life, i.e. from 1699-1741, he was a rather obscure Professor of Rhetoric at the University of Naples, and though he wrote and had published a number of works on philosophy and history during this time, these never had much general impact. So he never came to have an international reputation during his own lifetime and he never entered into the kind of debate with other philosophers which might have provoked him into trying to express himself more clearly and to remove the ambiguities from his thought.

I want, however, to mention two features of the intellectual life of his time which will help explain why Vico became interested in certain things and what it was he hoped he could do in these matters. The first is that the prevailing school of philosophy on the Continent was that of the Rationalists, i.e. followers of one kind or another of the philosophy of Descartes. Now, one of the main features of the thought of these philosophers was their search for certainty in knowledge and their decision to accept nothing as true which could not be shown to be absolutely certain. By and large the Rationalists had concluded that we could be certain about things if they were things whose behaviour was *absolutely determined* by certain causes. Therefore they thought that we could, for example, have knowledge in the field of the natural sciences or the material world, because that world was fully determined. Once one knew the causes of, say, condensation, evaporation, and precipitation one could formulate the laws which govern the fall of rain and, with knowledge of conditions on any particular day, one could predict with complete confidence whether or not it would rain or snow and so on.

But one field in which we could not have such certainty was that of history. And the reason for this was quite simple: the actions and deeds of human beings, which were the main part of history, were not fully determined. They were caused, certainly, but not determined. For their causes were the motives, and intentions and so on, of human beings; and the motives and intentions which determine the actions of human beings were not themselves determined, in the way that, say, the movements of the atoms which determined the movements of physical events were themselves determined. It may be true

that I go to the theatre because I want
to be entertained, but I don't have to
want to be entertained. So my going
to the theatre is not an absolutely,
or fully, determined occurrence. So
because of the importance of human
motives and intentions in determining
human actions, the latter lack the
fully deterministic character of events
in the world. Consequently when
an historian tells us that a certain
historical person did something for a
certain reason, we can never be sure
this is correct. An agent might always
have had any of a number of reasons
for his action and, as we cannot see
directly into other people's minds, and
particularly not into the minds of past
people, our explanations may always
be wrong. Consequently there can be
no knowledge of historical causes,

no science of history and no genuine knowledge of history.

At the same time, however, as the philosophers were coming to these gloomy conclusions about the possibility of historical knowledge, history itself, in the hands of historians, had taken some fairly important strides forward. The initial impetus for this had been the claims made by Luther in the Reformation and by his Catholic opponents in the Counter-reformation. These conflicting claims about the nature of the Christian religion had made it a matter of urgency to try to establish which parts of the Bible were true and how these sacred writings should be understood. So there had first been great improvements in developing a sound critical approach to the interpretation of the historical aspect of religious writings. This had then gained an impetus of its own and spread to the whole of historical enquiry, resulting in the great compilations of properly edited historical documents which first began to be produced in the 17th century.

But though there had been great advances in the critical approach to historical evidence the results of this still fell a long way short of Descartes' ideal. Historians were in a better position to establish *what* happened but they still couldn't go beyond this and explain *why* it happened for they still couldn't see how to gain certain knowledge of the minds of the agents in history. Consequently they couldn't establish the causes of historical change and formulate laws which stated what these were. So it still looked as though Descartes was right: in the natural sciences we could understand what happened because we could formulate laws giving the causes of things. In history we could not really understand what happened because we could never be certain that we knew what caused people to act in the ways they did.

Well, this position struck Vico as very odd, perhaps because he was both a philosopher and an historian. He began life as a follower of Descartes. But during his career he carried out a lot of research into history, particularly into Greek and Roman history, and it seemed to him that it was possible to have knowledge both of what happened and of why it happened. So, if, according to Descartes, such knowledge was impossible, there must be something wrong somewhere with Descartes' philosophy. Vico therefore began by asking himself what was

wrong with the way most other
philosophers were looking at history,
which was bringing them to these
wrong conclusions. And from this he
went on to formulate a theory about
the way they should try to approach
history and to show that if they did it
in this way, genuine knowledge could
be reached.

The first thing that Vico drew
attention to in the work of other
philosophers was that most of them
had a faulty conception of man. They
had defined history, quite correctly, as
consisting of the actions and deeds of
man, but because they had an incorrect
view of man's nature they had come
to the erroneous conclusion that one
could never know the causes of these
actions.

According to Vico their mistake
here had been to take man to be a

self-dependent entity, i.e. to think of each individual person as constituting an independent unity, the causes of whose activity were wrapped up within himself. Descartes, for example, had thought this, and this was what really lay behind his scepticism about historical knowledge. For Descartes had argued that since the causes of the actions of each person lay within himself, the only person who could be fully certain why he acted as he did on any particular occasion was that person himself. And *he* could know this because he had direct acquaintance, so to speak, with his own thoughts, whereas somebody else could only try to infer what these thoughts were and so could always be wrong about them. The first thing that Vico objected to in this view of man's nature was its anti-social character. It thought of individual human beings as being altogether too unaffected by each other and consequently attributed far too much importance to the role of free-will and, in general, purely individualistic factors in the explanation of their actions.

Now Vico, who was a devout Christian, did not want to deny that individuals had free-will but he thought of this as much more of a potentiality than an actuality and he thought that its actual operation was much exaggerated in the account Descartes gave. For the first thing that that account overlooked was that, though people's actions *were* governed by their motives, their beliefs about things and their attitudes to things, these motives, beliefs and attitudes, what I shall call the contents of human consciousness, were not formed by each individual for himself, but were largely inculcated into him by first, the type of family background he had, then the sort of education (i.e. both formal and informal education) he underwent, then by the sort of position he held in society. In other words, the free-will with which people were born was really only a freedom to come to have whatever beliefs about things and attitudes towards them they were trained and educated into having.

So the first way in which Vico wanted to modify current philosophical theories about man was by replacing the conception of man as a self-contained and self-determining being, by that of man as a socially conditioned entity, i.e. as a being who acquired a large part of what we would call his human nature in the course of being brought up in society.

Now it might seem that this point would be enough to enable Vico to reject Descartes' historical scepticism. For if an historian wanted to know what the motives were or aims behind the actions of any particular historical agent, he wouldn't be denied this because he couldn't gain access to the hidden interior of that person's mind. What he needed would be a correct account of the family, educational and social backgrounds that that individual had had and he would then be in a position to know and understand the attitudes and beliefs which that individual had come to possess and which determined his actions in any particular circumstances.

But, as a matter of fact, one really couldn't reject historical scepticism for this reason alone. For even if Vico's account were accepted, for each particular individual one would have to know the details of his own individual

family background, the sort of training
he received in this, then the details of
all the people he met in his social life,
what they said to him and so on. If he
wanted, for example, to understand
just what made, say, Henry II act as
he did towards Thomas Beckett, or
Beckett as he did towards Henry II, we
should have to have a whole account
of all the particular people who had
ever affected or influenced both men.
And, of course, the bulk of these people
leave little or no historical trace at all,
so that there would be no evidence
to enable us to know who and what
they were. So Vico would be no further
forward in his desire to show how we
could have historical knowledge.

Well Vico was not worried by
this objection because it was based
upon another faulty philosophical
conception: it thought of society

itself as being just an aggregate of individual people. But the truth, Vico argued, was that society had a certain structure which transcended, i.e. could not be explained by, the activities of individuals *qua* individuals and which, in fact, determined the nature of many of the beliefs and attitudes which individuals held in common. In fact, what Vico now produced was a theory of class structure, rather similar to that which Marx formulated, though Vico's theory predated that of Marx by just about a hundred years.

Now the essential point in this part of Vico's theory is that society, rather than being composed of an aggregate of individual people, really constituted a sort of unity, i.e. had a unified structure, and the sort of beliefs, attitudes, etc., which individuals have are to be explained by their place in this structure. To know, for example, the beliefs and attitudes which lay behind a certain course of action, one didn't need to have access to the hidden interior of an individual's mind, nor even to the details of all the specific experiences he had had. What one needed was some appreciation of the general nature of the various parts of society in which he moved. For example, his family background – if he lived in an agrarian society, were his family landowners or land workers? If he lived in a more commercial and urban society, was his family an employer of labour or did it itself consist of employed labour? And so on. Then, again, his education. If he lived in an agrarian society and, let's say, of a family of landowners, had his education, both formal and informal, been that of a typical land-worker, or had he, through some accident or circumstance, come to share in the education of a different part of society?

Now the reason why Vico thought that if we could know these details about an individual we could come to understand his activities, was that he thought that these social classes or groupings I've mentioned each had their own *guiding spirit* which impressed itself upon, or became a part of, anybody who was a member of them. Everybody who was a member of a landowning family, for example, would have a certain conception of his duties, his rights, his obligations, and so on. While everybody who was a member of a land-working family would also have a certain conception of his duties, rights, obligations, etc., but, of course, these would be different from those of the members of the land-owning family because of the different places or positions which the two kinds of family held *vis-à-vis* each other and in society as a whole.

So Vico presented a picture of the relation between the individual and society which was more or less the exact opposite of that presented by the rationalists. For the rationalists, individuals were self-sufficient and relatively independent entities, possessing faculties given them by God, which were more or less impervious to outside influence. Society was simply the sum of the relations they established externally between one another. For Vico the individual was through and through a society entity. Most of his main characteristics were inculcated into him by the teaching, training and experience he gained in his communal and social life. And the nature of these characteristics depended upon the general social structure and the place in this structure possessed by those groups in which the individual had his upbringing and lived his life.

Now Vico was not the first thinker to emphasise the fact that if we want to understand man we must think of him as a social being. This had been emphasised by a group of thinkers, or rather two groups of thinkers, who occupied a position which lay roughly half-way between those of Rationalists and Vico. These two intermediate groups of thinkers were the Natural Law theorists and the Social Contract theorists. I want to mention these here in order to show by comparison and contrast, just how extreme and radical Vico's view is and, also, in order to introduce a further most important aspect of his theory.

The point in which there is a genuine resemblance between Vico's views and the theories of the Natural Law and Social Contract schools is their common belief that men require not just a social context but a legally structured social context, if they are to live happily and harmoniously and to make the best use of the capacities and abilities which God has given them. The reason for this necessity was that they accepted the Christian view that man had fallen from his state of Grace and they interpreted this as meaning that he was ineradicably self-centred and egotistic in his basic nature. Therefore in a context in which there was no law, man would live only for the satisfaction of his own interests, and life would be bestial in the extreme. The law of the jungle would prevail. Now, thinking in this way, the problem had naturally arisen: 'How could it come about, as it obviously had, that a man of such rudimentary and bestial nature, should enter into social and legally enforceable relations with his fellow-men?', for the whole point of a legally structured society is that it prevents people from exercising some of their more antagonistic and destructive impulses. To this question, the two schools of thinkers had offered different answers. The Social Contract theorists had suggested that society was founded on a sort of initial contract which men were driven to agree to among themselves mainly because they were fearful of their ability to keep themselves alive in the non-social state, what they called the State of Nature. Fear therefore spurred them on to agree to give up some of their natural liberties, and to agree not to satisfy some of their natural desires and appetites, in order to set up an over-riding authority, the *State*, which would guarantee them some sort of stable social conditions, and some sort of protection from their stronger fellow-marauders. The particular kind of state which was formed depended upon the balance of power in the State of Nature. In the new social state, the stronger would still be stronger but at the same time they would be exposed to a series of legal checks in their exercise of their power. So the weaker would at least be free from dependence upon the *arbitrary* decisions of the stronger.

The Natural Law theorists agreed with this to the extent that they thought society existed to protect men from each other and to preserve their rights. But they rejected the suggestion that what these rights were depended upon some agreement or contract between men. Instead, they argued that these rights were men's inalienable, eternal possessions, i.e. something which, when men thought about them, they saw had to belong to all men, irrespective of who was the stronger, who the weaker and who could enforce his will on whom. So, on this view, life in a legally structured society, rested upon the fact that men had the power of Reason, and when they thought about things, they realised that all men had certain inalienable rights and the law had to be adapted to protect them in the exercise of these rights from the encroachments of their fellow men.

Well, Vico argued that there was something wrong with both these views. Let's take first the Social Contract view. According to this,

Civil Society was supposed to be the consequence of an agreement reached by men in which they gave up some privileges and freedoms in return for protection from the aggression of others. But, Vico argued, this gets the cart before the horse. For the ability to make agreements, to be able to give up something in return for something else, and to accept a whole way of life, i.e. social life, upon such a basis, is a very sophisticated ability, which men could only acquire through the teaching, training and development they receive in society. Society can't rest upon a contract, or agreement, for contracts and agreements presuppose a social upbringing. In this way, Vico argued, the Social Contract theorists had gone wrong because they had failed to realise how totally dependent man's abilities were on his social background and had tried to explain the social background by reference to some mythical prior abilities. So Vico's criticism here depended upon his taking a very much more radical view of the socially conditioned nature of man. Vico's view is so extreme that the question: 'How can man create society?' can't really arise. If Vico is right there can be no question of man's creating society because *he* is *its* product.

With regard to the Natural Law theorists Vico's criticism took a different form. As I've said, their view was that man lived in the context of a legally-structured society because, by use of his powers of reason, he realised that certain rights belonged to all men and that a legally-structured society was the only way of guaranteeing that all men enjoyed these rights. Now, in rejecting this view, Vico brought forward a point that goes beyond his position as I've so far described it. The Natural Law theorists attributed to man, i.e. to all men, two things: a set of inalienable rights, which therefore belong to all men *at all times*, and the faculty or power of *Reason*, which enabled men to recognise what these rights were. These rights, by the way, usually turned out to be such things as the right of self-preservation, and the right to private property, though there were some differences among theorists about some of them. But it doesn't really matter what they were for Vico rejected the whole idea that man had any inalienable rights and that man always had the faculty of Reason which enabled him to distinguish what these rights were. And he rejected both these conceptions because they failed to take into account not just the fact that man is socially conditioned but that he is *historically* conditioned.

To explain what Vico meant by historical conditioning I want to compare for a moment two different historical societies: say, Vico's own and that of early Rome. Now Vico lived in a relatively sophisticated age, one which had produced great lawyers, jurists, social analysts and so on. Consequently if one asked one of these sophisticated thinkers why he obeyed the law, why, for example, he didn't try to evade the law and get for himself certain things at the expense of others, he would, as I expect one would today, reply to the effect that he thought it was not *just* to do so, that it involved an infringement of other people's rights and so on. But if one pressed the question: 'But why do you retain this idea that others, i.e. anybody, has the rights?' the reply would probably be: 'A world in which there are no rights would be inconceivable to me. It's really part of the way things are,' i.e. the reply would be somewhat akin to that offered by the Natural Law theorists and in the end it would rest upon a *view of reality*, i.e. a view about the way things are. But suppose one could ask these questions of an ancient Roman. Suppose one began by saying: 'I've noticed you do a certain number of things because you take them to be to your own advantage. Why then don't you evade the laws for your own advantage?' A Roman might reply here: 'Because it infringes the rights of others.' But if pressed further with the question: 'Why don't you give up the idea that others have rights?' he wouldn't have said: 'Because it is inconceivable that people shouldn't have rights.' Here he would have replied: 'Because the Gods have ordained that we observe each other's rights.' And if further pressed with the question: 'Well, why don't you give up this belief in the Gods?' only then would he have replied: 'Because a world in which there are no Gods is inconceivable to me. I can't see how reality can be otherwise.'

Now the point of these two concocted examples is to show that, in the end, a large part of our beliefs is determined by the way we conceive reality and that in different societies reality is conceived differently. One society may have what is ultimately a theistic conception of reality and the kinds of rights, duties, etc., which are observed and enforced in that society will depend on how they construe the Gods' natures, commands and so on. Another society may have a materialistic conception and the kinds of rights and duties here observed and enforced will vary accordingly. The conception of reality is thus more basic to a society even than the kinds of laws and the sort of institutions it has. And once Vico had realised this he was able to reject the claim that there were some *natural* rights which belonged to all men and which all men could recognise. These rights would certainly be seen to be rights in a society with one conception of reality, but would not be recognised at all in a society with a different conception of reality.

Once he had realised this, however, Vico now went on to ask himself the question: 'What determines a society's conception of reality, and what causes the conception of reality in one society to differ from that in another?' Vico hit upon his answer to this question by asking himself another question.

As I said earlier, Vico was passionately interested in Greek and Roman history. Now, one of the questions which any good historian has to ask himself is: 'How was it possible for the Greeks and Romans to believe in their whole hierarchy of Gods?' For to us, today, these Gods seem utterly unbelievable figures and we find it difficult to see how otherwise intelligent people shouldn't find them as unbelievable as we do. To us they are figures of amusement and entertainment. How could it be, then, that to the Greeks, say, they were not, they were the very stuff of reality?

This, therefore, was a very real question for Vico. And while he was pondering it he suddenly hit upon the idea that perhaps the early Greek mentality was very like the mentality of a child today. For one of the characteristics of children is that they find it very difficult to draw the distinction we do between the imaginary and the real. It's not just that a child will sometimes be very frightened of something that we would say was purely the product of its own imagination, but that for a while children live wholly in a world which is an amalgam of what we teach them is real and what they imagine and take to be real. Well, Vico hypothesised, suppose there was a society in which people had the vivid power of imagination which children still have, and exercised this in their beliefs without somebody like ourselves trying to inculcate into them a different conception of reality. Wouldn't they then take everything they imagine to be real and wouldn't they then quite naturally and easily come to believe in the reality of a set of Gods who were really the products of their own imagination?

Once he had hit upon this idea Vico soon realised that if the beliefs of the early Romans and Greeks could be explained by saying that they had a much more imaginative and less rational nature than ours, the same must be true of all nations. For in their early history all nations had had their beliefs about Gods.

In this way Vico was led to develop his theory that the conception of reality held by a society depended upon what he called its basic, human nature, i.e. whether it was basically imaginative or rational and so on. Furthermore, since all nations had had an imaginative stage, he suggested that the basic human nature of any society went through a series of stages roughly akin to that which we see a child go through. Thus it would start with an imaginative stage (i.e. a stage in which all its main beliefs were determined by the exercise of an exceedingly vivid and powerful imagination). One of the main features of this age would be a fundamental belief in a world of Gods, and the character of all the institutions and practices of the age would depend upon this. For example, there would be a caste of priests to interpret the commands of the Gods. Kings would try to get divine sanction for their possession of their powers and so on. Vico called this age the poetic or theological age.

Next there would be what he called the heroic age. Here, the basic human nature would be starting to develop out of this completely imaginative stage.

People would try to reason about things but be unable to do so very well.

In particular they would be unable to reason in a general manner and all their institutions and laws would reflect this. They would be very precise, pedantic and particular and seem to us to be much more concerned with the details of things than with their spirit.

Finally from this there would develop the human age. Here people would at last be able to think about the nature of things and to adopt those social practices and institutions which were most likely to succeed in the light of their understanding of human nature and so on. Thus, at last, the legal system would centre round a perfect understanding of the concept of equity and all judicial procedures would be geared to this. The same would apply to the form of government, of economic organisation and so on.

One might have expected Vico's scheme to have stopped once this golden age is reached but as a matter of fact it didn't. For Vico took what is, in the end, a profoundly pessimistic view of human nature. Human achievements were the result of the historical development of society, and were largely communal in character. Human vices, however, were always the property of each individual person. They could be held in check only while the individual lived in fear of the pressures society could bring to bear against him and the retribution it could deal out. And they were most likely to be held in check when man conceived society as having objective characteristics, i.e. characteristics it held independently of himself, as he did, for example, when he thought it represented an order of existence established by the Gods. But when he came to see through this, when he came to see that society was not created by the Gods, for the latter were products of his own imagination, and that it was really only a human creation after all, the various mechanisms whereby society had regulated his own conduct, would lose their grip on him. He would see no reason why he should accept socially approved standards of conduct and morality, or why he should not indulge all his own self-centred vices. So, at the very moment when men appeared capable of setting up the perfectly organised society, one based upon reason and not imagination, man's vices would reassert themselves and begin to undermine his socially conditioned behaviour. This would reveal itself first of all in demands for increasingly democratic social, economic and political conditions and institutions, then in a demand for increasingly permissive forms of social behaviour and morality until finally the very notion of morality, of right and wrong, would disappear. Then there would be nothing left to force people to regulate their conduct and inhibit their anti-social desires. Sooner or later there would be some sort of enormous civil war and all man's social and cultural achievements would be destroyed. Man would be reduced to his initial state of bestiality from which he could only be rescued by a recurrence of the whole historical cycle.

In this way, therefore, Vico's theories finally came to rest with the production of the cyclical theory of history for which he is best known today. I've only mentioned the barest outline of it but Vico worked it all out in great detail.

He first of all examined the differences in the three stages in the development of human nature from which all else followed: he worked out first the differences between the imaginative, the heroic and the human mentalities, then he showed how from this there came three different conceptions of reality: the theistic, the semi-theistic and the humanist. Then he showed how institutions changed character through this historical sequence, for example how the family, which he took as the basic social unit, was organised in one way in the imaginative era, then in different ways in the heroic and human eras. Then he did the same for the economic and political institutions, the legal institutions, the religious institutions and so on. Finally he turned his attention to language and showed how it, too, altered its character as human nature developed through these consecutive phases. For example, in the human age, men distinguish between the literal use of language and its metaphorical use. But in the imaginative age there would be no such distinction. Men would use what we would now call metaphorical language but for them it would be a literal expression of reality as they saw it.

When we read in Homer the assertion, 'the magnet loves the iron', we think it is a metaphor. But, says Vico, this is wrong: in Homer it is intended as a literal expression of the truth, for in the imaginative age people cannot distinguish between the inanimate and the animate and so they attribute feelings to everything. This is therefore reflected in the character of their language.

However, though Vico worked this cyclical theory out in great detail I don't want to say anything more about it because it seems to me less important than the conception of historical causation which lies behind it. Consequently I would like to conclude by drawing out what seems to me some of the more interesting implications of the two main aspects involved in Vico's account. These are: the socially conditioned nature of man and the historically conditioned nature of society.

First I would like to point out the implication this theory has for our understanding of ourselves. If Vico is right, a certain belief about something, or a certain attitude towards something, is a phenomenon which is bound to occur whenever people live together in a certain kind of social situation and whenever society has reached a certain stage of historical or, for this is the way Vico treats this, mental development.

Now this conflicts with the way in which many of us ordinarily think of ourselves. It is probably true that most of us still think of ourselves in something like the way I suggested Descartes held, i.e. we think of our thoughts, our beliefs, our attitudes, as something which we produce individually from within ourselves. Of course, we don't believe we could think without, for example, being taught a language by means of which we can think. But we tend to look upon this language as an instrument which we can use well or badly according to our mental capacities, i.e. according to what is within each of us individually, and we think that the conclusions to which we come when we think about things depend *solely* upon these capacities which we have. The language itself, that which we are taught, is simply a sort of neutral instrument on this view.

Well, Vico doesn't want to deny that some people can think better than others, i.e. he doesn't want to deny that there are some differences between individuals. What he would deny, however, is the idea that language is a neutral instrument. For in his view the terms of a language are what is sometimes called 'theory-loaded', i.e. they are such that using them at all involves one in looking at things in a certain way. In being taught to use a language, we are not being taught how to use a neutral instrument in order to deal with things as they seem to us individually, we are being taught how to look at things, i.e. we are being taught how things should seem to us.

So when we are taught how to use a language, something pretty serious is going on.

We are not being handed an instrument simply to be used in accordance with capacities which God has given us or which can be explained by heredity, we are actually having certain very fundamental parts of our outlook formed for us. We are acquiring a part of our human nature. On this view, therefore, the effects of the sort of teaching we receive and the kind of upbringing we have are very much more drastic than we ordinarily think they are. What Vico is saying is that there are within society a number of mechanisms for teaching people what they ought to think and believe, how they ought to feel about things, what they ought to do about them and so on. And the differences between the thoughts, beliefs and feelings of different individuals are not to be explained by differences within their *inner* essences, so to speak, i.e. not by innate differences between the individuals themselves, but by the particular set of mechanisms to which they have been exposed in their upbringing. I know it is fashionable these days to say that the aim of education is to teach people *how* to think. But if Vico is right, this is hardly possible. Despite appearances, people are taught *what* to think.

The first thing Vico's theory suggests, then, is that we should pay very much less attention to individual factors in trying to understand ourselves and very much more attention to the general social situations in which we are brought up, in which we are taught not only how to think about things but also how to experience them.

The second thing I should like to point out is a corollary of the general view I have so far outlined. In the ordinary way we generally think of our beliefs as being in some general sense *rational*. By this I mean that if two people hold, as they often do, different beliefs about something, each will try to show that his is the correct belief to hold about it, by producing some reason which is alleged to *justify* the belief in question. And so, in general, when we find ourselves believing in one thing rather than another we tend to look for reasons which will justify our belief, i.e. demonstrate to us what makes it a correct belief to hold.

Again, however, according to Vico, this is not the proper approach to take. What we should do is to try to understand the social situation which can make it natural for such a belief to arise. In other words, we think of beliefs as rational and try to explain our acceptance of them by finding a reason to justify them. But in Vico's view they are socially conditioned, and what we should seek is not a justification for them but an account of the sort of social situation which can *cause* such a belief to arise, or of which it can be a part.

Now, perhaps some of us would be prepared to accept an account of this sort with regard to our moral, aesthetic and evaluative attitudes towards things. For example, we might be prepared to accept that the ways in which we think about the general political situation in Britain, the terms in which we think of this sort of problem, are really to be explained by the social and economic class structure of the nation. This conditions the sorts of view that are possible for us, while the actual view any of us takes depends upon the view our upbringing has conditioned us to take. And perhaps the same applies to our views on morality. We might, as I said, accept this because in these matters people do have different views and, as it is obvious that not all these views can be correct, it seems obvious also that the explanation why people adopt them can't be that they perceive the truth of them.

But what about our beliefs about factual truths? What about our belief that, say, the sun is 92 million miles away? Here, surely, is a belief we all share and surely we share this because science can *prove* that it is true. Here, then, is a belief which is shared by people of all backgrounds, so that one can't explain the arising of a belief like this by looking at the different social contexts in which people live. Moreover, here is a belief the truth of which *can* be justified, even though we perhaps couldn't all do the justifying ourselves. Isn't this, therefore, something which can't be explained by the kind of view Vico is putting forward?

Well, I don't think it is. Although we think we can prove a fact of this sort we can only do so by assuming the standards of proof, and the kinds of scientific theory, current to our time, i.e. current within a given society. But the second of Vico's points was that a society is historically conditioned. Consequently the kinds of scientific theory, and the standards of proof, it accepts are conditioned by the mental development of the people who are involved in it. *Given* our theories and standards, we have no option, if we can follow through the proof, but to accept that the sun is 92 million miles away. But given the theories and standards of another age, not only would such a thing have been entirely unprovable but the very proposition would have seemed silly. To a primitive, the suggestion that the sun is 92 million miles away would have seemed as silly and incredible as to us does the suggestion that it is about the size of a florin and is just out of reach in the sky. What makes one credible and the other incredible at any given time is not the obvious truth of one or another view but the theories and standards current at the time which render one or the other obviously true to someone brought up to accept them.

'Well, that's all right,' one might say, 'and we know that our theories and standards are the correct ones, therefore we know that the sun is 92 million miles away and is not the size of a florin.'

But if Vico is right, that our theories and standards are the correct ones is precisely what we can't know. All we can say is that they are the kinds of theories and standards which a society at a certain stage of historical conditioning will come to develop and they will be assumed by all the reasoning performed within that society. But that, as they stand in this century, last century or the next century, any of these theories and standards have superior claims to correctness over any others, is something which can never be shown. Next century or the century after people may look back at our science and our beliefs and think, 'How quaint. How could they have believed that?' just as we look back and think,

'How quaint. How could they believe the sun was just on the horizon?'

So on Vico's view, though there may be, in fact must be, some beliefs which all members of a society share, this isn't enough to give them any claim to objective truth nor to show that they are not also as conditioned as the beliefs about which we differ. In fact, this is one of the real values of the study of history for us. If Vico is right, where we have a belief which seems to us obviously true, and which seems to all of us obviously true, we can come to see the conditioned nature of that belief only by studying history, or studying other societies at a different stage of historical development, and finding that in other historical times such a belief would have been either incredible or even inconceivable. Then, from the contrast, we shall be able to put our own most deeply held beliefs into a correct perspective and see them for what they are – the products of a long historical process.

Now this kind of historical determinism is something which people find very uncomfortable to face up to, and philosophers have made a number of attempts to show that there is something unacceptable about it. For example, one objection which has been raised against it is that the theory is self-refuting. For if we accept that we are all so conditioned by our historical heritage that we can never know the absolute truth about anything, what are we to say about the theory which states that this is so? i.e. if there is no such thing as the objective truth, can the theory which involves this claim itself be claimed to be true?

Karl Marx, for example, considered this kind of objection against his particular brand of historical determinism and took it as a very serious objection. To defeat it he tried to argue that his theory, i.e. the theory of historical materialism, could be shown to be true because it involved a method, i.e. the scientific method, which was not itself the product of historical conditions and did not involve the application of historically conditioned modes of thought. Well, this is a most inadequate reply to the objection, for a little study of history would soon show that the methods of science have varied widely over the ages – after all, witch doctors apply what is for them a certain conception of scientific method. The methods which we accept, today, or those which Marx accepted last century, are different from those of the past and may well be different from those of the future. So, if scientific method is historically conditioned one can't defend the objectivity of a certain scientific theory by appealing to the method it uses.

But though Marx's reply fails to meet the objection, it seems to me that the objection really has very little force in it. It may well be that, if Vico's theory, or another like it, is accepted, we have to accept also that it is itself the product of its age and that it can't therefore be thought of as offering an objective truth. At best it states the truth as we, *given* the historical past which has conditioned us, see it. But that still leaves it in a better condition than other theories we might produce which fail even to do this. So the theory isn't shown to be self-refuting because it can't be objectively true – it can still remain the one which most recommends itself to people at our stage of historical and conceptual development. In other words, the admission that a theory does not contain the final truth does not imply that it may not be the best theory we can produce and the one we ought to accept. At the same time one would not want to deny that the recognition of his fact does put the theory, and all our thinking about things, in a certain perspective, as I have earlier tried to explain.

The attack against Vico's kind of historical determinism has sometimes taken another form. It is often claimed that such a view is refuted by the *facts* of history themselves. For history shows that the personal qualities of certain individuals have been, to say the least, very important influences in determining the course of events.

LEON POMPA, M.A., PH.D.

For example, had there been no such individual as Hitler, with his particular qualities of character, there would have been no Second World War. Or had there been no such person as Churchill, with his particular qualities of character, Germany would have won that war. Now, in making this suggestion, it is not being proposed that, say, Hitler was the sole cause of the war. It is recognised that Hitler could only bring about the war *given* certain already existent general conditions, such as the economic and social situation in Germany, the spirit of international hostility and the mutual suspicion which was an aftermath of the First World War, the fear of Russian Communism which at least acted as a check upon the willingness of some countries to declare war upon Germany and so on. But, the objection goes, these conditions were not themselves enough to bring about the war. What was equally necessary was for there to be somebody in a position, so to speak, to press the trigger, and only a person of Hitler's unique blend of fanaticism, megalomania, utter ruthlessness, and so on, could have done this. So, without such an individual as Hitler there would have been no war. But, the objection finally states, it is simply an historical accident that such a person should be around at the time, and that he should get into the one position in which he could have wielded such an influence on events. For if the appearance of a man with the personal qualities of character of Hitler in Germany in the first half of the 20th century was determined, it was certainly not determined by such factors as those adduced by Vico in his theory, which have all to do with the general structure of a society and the general modes of thought and belief which prevail in it. In this way, therefore, it is argued that, although the context in which historical events occur is important in helping to explain their character, it is never possible wholly to do away with the decisions of individuals and there are in part, at least, dependent upon the character of individuals, characters which are not determined in the same way as the more general context. So Vico's account of the causes of historical change is inadequate.

In reply to this objection I would like to make two points. First I would like to say that Vico himself would probably have accepted it to a certain extent. For, as I said earlier, he did not want to say that the personal qualities of individuals were completely unimportant. For example, he himself was a great admirer of Augustus and he believed that had it not been for certain qualities of character which Augustus had, the decline of Rome would have taken place even more quickly than it did. Certain qualities of Augustus's character, however, enabled him to *delay* the eventual collapse of Rome, but that's as far as it goes. The collapse came in the end, just the same. And that is because it was made inevitable by conditions operating at a much more fundamental level than those which can be influenced by the activities of anyone man. On this view, therefore, the success or the failure of the plans and ventures of the great depends upon the extent to which the aims involved in these are in harness with the underlying and quite inevitable general changes. The great individual has some small amount of manoeuvre left him, but whether his exercise of this results in something of relatively permanent or something of merely temporary effect in history depends entirely upon whether what he does is in conformity with the inevitable pattern of change or whether it is in conflict with it.

Having said this, however, I should like to turn to my second point, which is that, though Vico undoubtedly did make this allowance about the way great men can affect the course of history, I don't see why it should be thought of as an exception to a fully deterministic account. In this objection as I stated it, it is treated as an exception because the qualities of character of individuals are claimed not to be *fully* determined by the individual's social environment. What, for example, was different in the social and historical environment in which Hitler was brought up, which would have to be responsible, say, for his megalomania, from that in which thousands of his non-megalomaniac contemporaries were brought up? And if we can't produce such an element in the social and historical environment then we can't say that Hitler's character was fully determined by social and historical conditions. And if we can't say that his character was fully determined by such conditions then neither can we say that those events which turned upon his discussions and activities were.

Now what this objection seems to overlook is that it is, strictly, misleading to talk as though the actions of anyone individual are effective simply because they are *his* actions alone. Any ruler, no matter how absolutist or dictatorial, has to have some support for his policies.

When he decides upon a policy or tries to have it effected, he has to persuade some people, at least, that this is what ought to be done. Hitler didn't act in isolation and in the face of the wishes of everybody in Germany. Somebody had to go along with him in it all, and his policies had to have some appeal to certain parts of German society. Again, Churchill was effective as a leader in the last war because what he said and did struck a chord in the attitude of the British people. In a different people, or at a different time, the response might have been very different and Churchill consequently would have had none of his present fame. So, if we say that Hitler was a megalomaniac and that only a megalomaniac could have done what he did, we have to recognise that his megalomania (if that's what it was) was not a purely idiosyncratic feature but something which could develop in some fairly large section of the German people in the social and historical situation in which they were. Likewise, if we say that only a patriot could do what Churchill did, again we have to recognise that he *shared* in a sentiment which was held by a large part of the population of Britain.

But once this fact has been recognised, it seems to me to be increasingly improbable that the explanations or the actions of Hitler or Churchill are to be found in purely individual factors. When one has found the social and historical conditions which produced the patriotism which Churchill shared with the British public, or which produced the megalomania in which Hitler and many Germans shared, one will have found the underlying reasons why history took the general course it did. I come back to Vico's original point, therefore, that when individuals have certain qualities of character and outlook, and so on, this is to be thought of as their coming to share in certain social phenomena – these qualities, attitudes, beliefs and so on, are the products of people's being involved in certain social relationships in certain social and historical circumstances. And if we want to understand either ourselves or the reasons why our activities take the forms they do, or why history takes the course it does, it is to these areas we must direct our attention.

A list of all the monographs to be published in the series:

An Eye to the Future
Dr. Alexander King, Dr. Martin Holdgate, Eugene Grebenik, Dr. Kenneth Mellanby, George McRobie

East and West, Today and Yesterday
Sir Stephen Runciman, Patrick O'Donovan, Peter Brent, Sir Roger Stevens, Nirad C. Chaudhuri, Iris Butler, Prof. G.M. Carstairs, Richard Harris

Science and the Paranormal
Leonard Lewin, D.Sc.

Sufic Traces in Georgian Literature
Katharine Vivian

Rembrandt and Angels
Michael Rubinstein

Biological and Cultural Evolution
Mary Midgley

The Age of Anxiety: a Reassessment
Malcolm Lader

Goethe's Scientific Consciousnes
Henri Bortoft

The Healing Within: Medicine, Health and Wholeness
Robin Price

A Clash of Cultures: The Malaysian Experience
David Widdicombe, Q.C.

Evaluating Spiritual and Utopian Groups
Arthur J. Deikman, M.D.

The Crusades as Connection: Cultural transfer
during the Holy Wars
Contributed by Cultural Research Services

Baptised Sultans: The contribution of Frederick II
of Sicily in the transfer and adaptation of Oriental
ideas to the West
Contributed by Cultural Research Services

Brain Development During Adolescence and
Beyond
Dr. Sarah-Jayne Blakemore

Collective Behaviour and the Physics of Society
Philip Ball

Counter-Intuition
Dr. Kevin Byron

Music, Pleasure and the Brain
Dr. Harry Witchel

Fields of the Mind
Dr. Rupert Sheldrake

Why do we leave it so late?
David Canter

Scheherazade and the global mutation of teaching
stories
Robert Irwin

Consciousness, will and responsibility
Chris Frith

Extraordinary Voyages of the Panchatantra
Ramsay Wood